Forty-Cent Tip

Stories of New York City Immigrant Workers

BY THE STUDENTS OF THREE NEW YORK PUBLIC INTERNATIONAL HIGH SCHOOLS

Introduction by Marcelo M. Suárez-Orozco

Edited by What Kids Can Do

NEXT GENERATION PRESS

Providence, Rhode Island

Printed in Hong Kong by South Sea International Press Ltd.
Distributed by Next Generation Press, Providence, Rhode Island

ISBN 0-9762706-4-1
CIP data available.

Book design by Sandra Delany.

Next Generation Press, a not-for-profit book publisher, brings forward
the voices and vision of adolescents on their own lives, learning, and
work. With a particular focus on youth without privilege, Next
Generation Press raises awareness of young people as a powerful
force for social justice.

Next Generation Press, P.O. Box 603252, Providence, RI 02906
www.nextgenerationpress.org

10 9 8 7 6 5 4 3 2 1

Contents

Preface

THE PHOTOS AND STORIES HERE ARE THE WORK of sixty-seven students and teachers at three of New York City's small public schools for newcomers—Brooklyn International High School, Manhattan International High School, and International High School at LaGuardia Community College. Their work is part of a larger initiative called Student Research for Action, sponsored by our nonprofit What Kids Can Do, with support from the Bill & Melinda Gates Foundation.

Powerful learning occurs, WKCD holds, when young people and their adult mentors put their minds and muscle into an issue that matters greatly to them. Link their investigation to the creation of a public product, aimed at heightening awareness and encouraging action, and the learning grows even more remarkable.

Forty-Cent Tip backs up these beliefs. The narratives and images collected by its student authors mean the world to them, and it shows. They tell of relatives, friends, and neighbors who are recent immigrants like themselves, and for whom the American dream often remains just that. Sometimes for the first time here, parents have spoken to children of their disappointments and hardships. No matter how bitter their experiences, their words also ring of hope, persistence, courage, and love.

Many of the students who carried out this project have been in this country for only a year or two. As they sharpened their interview skills, worked their cameras, translated and transcribed their taped interviews, then turned them into narratives, their commitment to the project only deepened. At each school, students and teachers proudly exhibited their photographs and stories for all to see. More quietly, they sorted through the lessons gathered about justice and equity in the American workplace.

At WKCD, we also confronted some of those hard realities, as we brought these stories and images into published form. Some of the students and those whom they interviewed suffered serious apprehension about the consequences of making their identities known; we made the difficult decision, therefore, to omit specific attributions for each story and picture. Although filled with admiration for the hard work of both the students and their subjects, we want to avoid at all costs the risk that they would suffer for making it public. Instead, we have named in the acknowledgments all students who participated in this project, giving special mention to those whose photographs and texts we selected for publication.

In tribute to the work presented here, we have also given it our most careful editorial attention. In a number of instances, we chose not to present a photograph with the story of its subject, or vice versa, so that the book would include only the strongest submissions. While respecting the words of students and their subjects, we did edit the texts for length and organization, as we would for any adult author.

Rosa Fernández, our summer intern who is herself a recent graduate of Manhattan International High School and now a junior at Wellesley College, put her heart and mind into the book's development, and it shines because of her. Kathleen Cushman coached the students in the early stages of their writing and edited the pieces selected for *Forty-Cent Tip*. The collaborating teachers and artists at all three schools supported the project every step of the way. On each of us, the project has had its own profound effect. We hope it will open new doors to you as well.

Barbara Cervone
What Kids Can Do, Inc.
September 2005

Introduction
by Marcelo M. Suárez-Orozco

Courtney Sale Ross University Professor of Globalization and Education
Co-Director, Immigration Studies at NYU

THIS MOVING BOOK CAPTURES WITH CLARITY AND ELOQUENCE the bittersweet realities of life in the mythical city of immigrants. It is unique, telling the tale of immigration—its dreams and ambitions, heartbreaks and losses—with an emotional intimacy and authenticity rare in the more academic and scholarly literatures of immigration. It is beautiful, the product of the hard work, discipline, and creativity of youth who are themselves children of immigration. They bear witness to the enormous hardships their parents, relatives, and friends endured in their uncertain journey to the new land. That journey is paved with obstacles, frustrations, and sacrifices of biblical proportions, where immigrants find rewards but also experience disappointments. Finally, the book is gratifying, to be read and reread. It reveals important truths about immigration. The reader will be deeply affected by these powerful vignettes of love and work.

"Love and Work," after all, was Sigmund Freud's famed formula for a happy life: If one can love and work, one should be a happy person. The good Doctor's wise words encompass much that is relevant to understanding today's migration stories. "Love and work" is the best explanation for much of today's human migration. The search for better opportunities (work and wages) in wealthier countries, often to support relatives left behind, is the enormous ethical engine of care driving world migration. And what an efficient engine it is: We are in the midst of the largest wave of migration in human history, with well over 175 million souls living beyond their countries of their birth.

The United States is one of a handful of advanced post-industrial democracies in the world that can claim immigration as both their history and their destiny. Human migration made the United States the country it is today. The first important migration led to the earliest known human settlements of North America by native peoples over 12,000 years ago. The second important migration took place during the sixteenth and seventeenth centuries, when Spanish, Dutch, and Swedish colonists settled in what we now call Florida, New Mexico, New York, and Delaware. English colonists settled in Jamestown (1607) and the Pilgrims seeking religious freedom settled in Plymouth Plantation (1620). Then there were the mass kidnappings and involuntary transfer of millions of African slaves against their will, constituting the greatest involuntary migration in history. Between the end of the Napoleonic Wars and the first decade of the twentieth century, over 50 million people emigrated from the Old World and settled in North and South America. The story of that great human migration is the stuff of myth, chronicling the great travails and triumphs of millions of mostly poor, illiterate peasants—Germans, Irish, Italians, Eastern Europeans, and others becoming, over time and across generations, prosperous, loyal, and proud Americans.

By the mid-1960s, we began the most recent chapter in the long migration saga that is the history and destiny of the United States. It built powerful momentum by the 1970s and 1980s, peaking in the 1990s when the U.S. saw over a million new immigrants—legal and undocumented—arrive each year. By 2000, the U.S. had over 34 million immigrants—the largest number in its history, though proportionately less than in previous eras of large-scale immigration. Today's immigrants are no longer Europeans, but hail from all over the world, with Latin Americans, Asians, and Caribbeans leading the way. New York City, the mythical metropolis of global migration, is again contemplating a future where immigrants will play a vital role in its economy, politics, and culture: Children from about 200 countries around the world now attend the New York City schools.

But these large historical and demographic patterns are constituted of millions of human stories, each irreducible to dry statistics and social science abstractions. In *Forty-Cent Tip* we hear the voices of the army of invisible hands toiling at the wrong end of the American rainbow: cleaning offices and homes, cooking and delivering meals, washing clothes, doing dishes, and serving meals, often under appalling circumstances. A former businessman from China tells of working endless hours in a dangerous warehouse job until his hands become numb. A dentist from Colombia tells of working in the shadowy world of illegal dentistry. A Bangladeshi woman shares her struggle to make 100 packets of "somucha" a day, each packet with fifty somucha inside. You do the math.

Forty-Cent Tip does more than simply describe the endless routines in the "dirty, dangerous and demanding jobs" that rich countries like the United States summon immigrants to do. It also chronicles the eternal search for dignity, respect, and solidarity with loved ones. The immigrant story is foremost a story of hope and optimism under adverse conditions of loss, displacement, and cultural disorientation. It is a story of dreams and the enormous sacrifices people make so that the next generation can achieve a better place under the sun. It is the most human of stories.

OCTOBER 2005

Forty-Cent Tip

My Feet on the Ground

Office cleaning person

COUNTRY OF ORIGIN: Colombia

AN EMPTY OFFICE MAKES ME WONDER: Is my life as silent and isolated as my job? I am part of a doctor's office. That sounds good, hah! But I am just there after working hours, to clean the dust and vacuum the floor.

The day I left Colombia, I did it without regrets. Even though I worked in a pharmaceutical company in my country, I knew that here I would have to do any reasonable job that came my way. Now I work for a cleaning company, in the doctor's office and at a ballet academy. My benefits amount to only one, having a stable job. My salary is twelve dollars an hour, and I work seven hours per day. It is not a lot of money, but if you see my work, that is what it's worth.

I spend my afternoons working, and I know that I am not part of my daughters' life. I barely see them. That is my greatest sacrifice: being there for them, but not physically as I wish.

Now I am not killing myself, working long schedules and working on holidays as I used to. My work keeps life busy while I wait for my youngest daughter to graduate from high school so I can move, probably to another country or state. After sacrificing myself most of my life for my daughters, it is time for me to take a break. Eternal vacations, here I come. Five years from now, those will be my words.

I dream that one of my daughters will be a dentist in a faultless huge office like this, surrounded with advanced technology, working with Americans that are respectful and helpful. But for now, I just clean and clean. Hopes and dreams keep my feet on the ground. I do not speak as much English as you do, but I understand more than you imagine.

Shirts Through the Night

Clothing factory worker

COUNTRY OF ORIGIN: China

BEFORE I CAME HERE, I WORKED IN CHINA AS A TEACHER. All I had to do was teach all those wonderful kids and see their smiles every day. It was like living in heaven, having all those cute angels around you. I thought my life would stay like that forever.

Unfortunately, my life changed. I got divorced from my husband. My happy family broken, I thought I needed a new life. My two sisters are in America, so I decided to come and look for the roads covered in gold. I left China, my daughter, and my past on a rainy day in November 1996, when I was thirty years old.

I would like to be a teacher again, but my education doesn't help here, where everybody speaks English. I've been making clothing since I was really young, so working in a clothing factory became my only choice. Now I have been doing that for almost ten years.

The working conditions are really bad. More than fifty people, male and female, use the same dirty, disgusting bathroom, and I have to bring my own toilet paper. My co-workers are all strangers; nobody remembers each other after they leave the factory. Our pay depends on the quality and quantity of the clothing. If any worker is not fast or professional enough, they get fired, and we have no benefits.

Once, the boss asked me to finish over one hundred T-shirts to be sent out the next day. I couldn't say no. I stayed in the factory working for ten more hours, cursing at my boss when I was the only one still there around three a.m. As soon as I finished the last piece, I fell asleep, right in my chair in the factory, until the first worker came in the next day.

At my age, I don't have much hope for the future. I just want my check to come on time. I got remarried here and have my second seed. He is only four years old, and I'm now in my forties. As I get older and can't work anymore, I can't be sure that I can continue to feed him. So now I put all my hopes for that in my daughter, who I finally brought over from China. I work so hard because I don't want her to bring her own toilet paper to work. I want her life to be more colorful than mine. That will be the happiness I have been looking for.

Forty-Cent Tip

Waiter

COUNTRY OF ORIGIN: Colombia

Olé! olé!" I hear the sound of people screaming for the bull killer as I help the poor bull that got hurt. Then, "Eduardo, come clean table number one!" Oh, I'm back to reality. It gets me mad. In my country, I was a well known veterinarian, but here I'm just a waiter who has no name. One day my name is Carlos, another day Oscar, taking on other people's identities, because to the government I don't exist. Like the weather in this city, every three months I change. I'm undocumented—so what? I still get food on my table.

I'm a dreamy person; my mind goes off to different places at the wrong time. When I'm at work, my mind is back in Colombia. Here, I have to clean tables and be nice to people. In Colombia, I helped animals and screamed at people for how they took care of them. Back in Colombia, I tried to save animals from dying. Here I serve dead animals on plates. It's funny, if you think about it; you don't know how good you had it until you lose everything.

I came to this country to make more money. I remember when my mother used to tell me, "In the U.S. you can find a job on every corner. It's the only place where everybody is equal; it's the promised land, *mijito*." Mom, I love you, but that was the biggest lie anybody ever told me. I have been here four years, and I still don't see the promised land. Yeah, you get money, but nobody tells you about the hard work of an immigrant, and people making fun of your English. You can never get respect if you come from another country. For a person who has graduated from university, it's hard to think you will be working at a restaurant in New York City.

Don't get me wrong, my job is okay. Except on the days when little kids are here, leaving the biggest messes ever. Or the old guy that always sits at table three, who wants his glass to look like thin air, as if it wasn't even there. He always asks for the same meal, a steak with a Coke. It costs $39.60, and he leaves on the table forty bucks. You do the math, to see how much I get for a tip.

But a job is a job. At least I have food and a very small home with one room. So thanks, Mom, for these ideas of coming here for a better life. It is good—but no better.

My Beautiful Life

Restaurant worker

COUNTRY OF ORIGIN: Ecuador

JOSÉ! JOSÉ! GO FIX TABLE TWO!" That is what I hear every day, cleaning, cleaning, and more cleaning. My life is beautiful—of course, not as beautiful as I would like, but I can't complain.

I started working as a kid, back in my country, Ecuador. I was very poor and my parents didn't have money to give me. I was probably seven years old when I went out to the streets to sell pineapple slices. Usually in a day I would make 40 to 50 pesos and give my mom 30 pesos. It was hard work for a kid that age.

As I grew up, I went from cleaning people's shoes to carrying groceries. At fifteen, I was driving a truck. You might wonder, why so young? But that was my everyday life.

I met my wife and along came my first child, and then I had to make the hard decision to come to this country, leaving my wife, my child, and everything behind.

I came with nowhere to stay, and no one to pick me up from where I was left. I took a taxi and wandered around the city. The taxi driver asked me, "Are you lost?" I said, "How can I know, if I just got here?" We talked for long hours, and then he offered me a little room in his apartment until I found something better and a job. I considered myself the luckiest man in the world.

The days passed, and I started working in an Italian restaurant in Manhattan. I worked there as a dishwasher for almost six years, and then the owner took me to another restaurant as a busboy. It was much easier work, nicer than washing dishes and being in the kitchen all the time.

After fourteen years I know every corner of this restaurant like the palm of my hand, and sometimes I wonder why I am still here. Thank God, I haven't got injured; I have no benefits. But in these years of working and saving, I have been able to bring my family here, buy two houses and two cars, and, best of all, have another daughter, who made my whole life complete. All my sacrifices have been worth it, because now I have a beautiful life. My only wish is that my kids graduate and become someone important in this country, and that they work in a office—not like me.

Shattered by Reality

Hotel housekeeper

COUNTRY OF ORIGIN: China

MOST PEOPLE HAVE DREAMS, AND SO DO I. My dream is to become an artist. I wanted to go somewhere in Europe, such as Paris or London. However, when my mom called me from the U.S and said that she could bring me from China to New York to live with her, I chose to go. At the time, it sounded pretty exciting and totally strange to me. I thought I would like the challenge of a new life.

Time passes fast; it's been two years since I came here. I have been telling myself to wake up since my first day in this country. I was living a life of the imagination, and the reality is cruel. I work as a housekeeper in a hotel in Manhattan.

I work twenty hours a week, on Saturday and Sunday. The first day was the worst; they would only give me twenty dollars, but the boss told me it would be better later on. He showed me how to use the tools, and my first job was to clean the bathroom. I was not allowed to wear gloves while working. I cleaned really carefully, but when the boss came back and checked it, he told me to do it again. I did not even eat my lunch on that day, because the boss told me to clean the same place over and over again. When I got back home that night, the first thing I did was wash my hands. My mom cried, because she had never seen me exhausted like that. I did not even have strength to breathe.

The same thing continued, even after I had worked there nearly six months. As time passes, my boss blames us every day for every single thing. Nobody can read his temper, he always releases it on us. One day he was really mad and said all the bad words to me. I am not a machine, I am a normal person, why should I stand there and listen to what he said? So I made the decision to quit. My English skills are good enough to help me find another job.

Between here and China, I choose China, because there I had a dream. Here, I gave up my dream because I don't have any time to make it come true. All I think about is how to make more money to support my family. Where's my dream? It is shattered by reality.

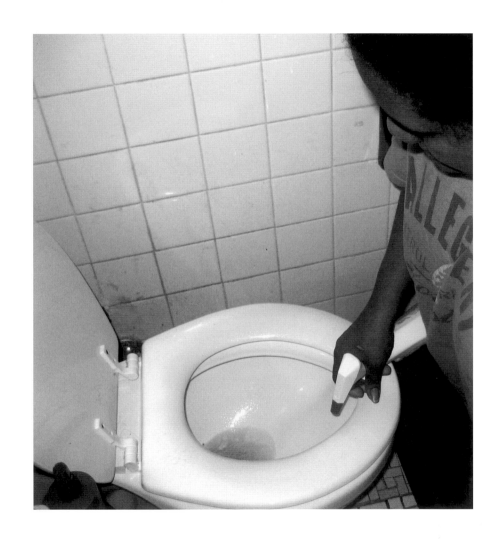

Chronicles of a Female Cab Driver

Taxi driver

COUNTRY OF ORIGIN: Dominican Republic

WHEN I CAME FROM THE DOMINICAN REPUBLIC to the United States about eight and a half years ago, I thought things were going to be much easier. In my country I worked as a secretary for a law firm. When I came to this country, I started waiting tables in a restaurant. It was very difficult and tiring, ten or sometimes even thirteen hours a day. It caused me back pain and my feet were often numb.

In 1999 I began to work as a taxi driver. You are your own boss, but it is a dangerous and risky job. You need to pay attention to the base radio, to traffic lights, to people crossing the street, to the police, to passengers coming up on the streets. When I began, seven or eight taxi drivers had been murdered in my neighborhood, but I never had the time to think that something bad was going to happen to me. My main bad experiences have been when people don't pay me, or when the radio is stolen. In order to eat or go to the bathroom, we have to find a secure parking space; if we can't, we keep on working, which causes health complications. The job also causes back and foot pain, and I began to suffer from vertigo, a lack of oxygen to the brain caused primarily by stress.

I started by working during the day, as I didn't know much about the city and the street names. After I felt more confident, I started to work at night; during the day, I do my chores. I work from four p.m. to midnight. I am never in the streets working after that, because I consider it dangerous to work late at night.

Taxi drivers can sometimes take a day off, but that one day means less money. We need to work seven days a week to pay for the rented car, gasoline, parking, and radio base, plus the common extra of a police ticket once a day. I have always worked on Christmas and January 31, when taxi drivers want to be with their families. We must sacrifice that, because those days are when you earn the most money.

When one can't manage easily with the language, people tend to get angry and get out of the car. Some women who call to get a cab don't want to get in the cab when they see a woman driver. Most men support me; they even think that it is beautiful to see a woman driving a taxi. They sometimes fear that we may panic and lose control, but statistically, men have more accidents than women.

Vendor Rolling

Ambulant vendor

COUNTRY OF ORIGIN: Peru

MY STORY IS NOT QUITE LIKE EVERYONE ELSE'S. I am one of the few special immigrants in this country, because of my disability. I was born in Peru in 1962, and five years ago I had an accident that left me handicapped. I have been in this country for three years. I cannot walk, so it is very difficult for me to get a job.

Back in Peru, I had independent jobs in business and commerce. Here I just roll around the streets as an ambulant vendor. I sell things—artworks and jewels that I've learned to make myself—to make a little money. I work six hours a day, seven days a week, and I make about $30 each day.

I know the very basics of English, and I can somewhat understand it when people talk, but I cannot have a conversation myself. If I could, I would have a better job; there are office jobs where handicapped people like me can work and get benefits. I am documented, so I do have health insurance, and that's what sustains me here. I am self-employed, but I don't report my income.

I don't have an ambulant vendor's license, so my job is risky; many times the police stop me. Whenever I see a policeman, I hold the items I sell in my lap and cover them with a cloth, or I just put them in a bag and roll on the streets as if I have done nothing. But I get caught anyway, and I get tickets that I cannot afford to pay. Then I am taken to court, and I have to go out there and make some more money illegally to pay those fees.

I like my job because I get to meet all kinds of people. Many are friendly and I chat with them. This way I make clients who like my craftwork, and since it's cheap, they tend to buy it. But one time, two men deceived me by offering to sell me a recording camera. We came to an agreement and they went to supposedly get the camera, which was in a bag. When I opened the bag to check, I found a toy. I looked up, but the men took off with my money; they knew I wasn't able to get up and do anything about it. There was nothing I could do but move on.

I don't make as much money as I would like, but it's better than what I was making in Peru, and there it's hard to be as mobile. I have talent and experience in selling things; one of my goals is to open up a store so I have something stable. I still haven't reached the American dream. But I am advancing, and little by little, I know I will get there.

An Anxious Life

CD seller

COUNTRY OF ORIGIN: China

THE LAST JOB I HAD WAS SEWING IN A CLOTHING FACTORY, which is at least a safe place to work. But after 9/11, many clothing factories were forced to close. There were not enough clothes for us to sew, and sometimes we only sewed two days a week. I only got one or two hundred dollars a week. How could I feed my family and myself? I have only learned a few sentences of English.

Now I sell pirated CDs in beauty shops, bars, restaurants, and laundromats. I know this is illegal, but I don't have a choice. By selling CDs, at least I can survive here.

I can only sell them secretly, and the work is very hard. I carry a bag of CDs and hold some in my hand. Every time I go into a shop, thousands of times a day, I say to the customers, "CD, CD—you want it?" I have to walk into many shops. Sometimes the owners don't want me to sell pirated CDs there, so I have to look for another shop. While I am selling, I have to look around to make sure there are no police nearby. If they see me, they will catch me and put me in jail. Last week, I was carrying a lot of CDs on the street and I saw a policeman walk by my side. I thought he would catch me, so I ran to escape. As a woman, I don't run fast, so I had to use all my energy. Luckily, he didn't catch me, but I cannot be sure about the next time. They should understand how hard a life I have.

On the average, I can earn $100 a day. If it's a rainy day, then I won't go out to sell, because not many people go out on rainy days. These days are my holidays—or I could also say they are my bad days, because I can't earn money.

El Barrio

Hotel housekeeper

COUNTRY OF ORIGIN: *Panama*

I DIDN'T WANT TO DO THIS JOB; I wanted to be a gynecologist or a nurse. I didn't accomplish my dream, because I got pregnant; I had to go to work instead of college. I came to the United States because of the opportunity for a better job and a better life for my kids. The major obstacle was my papers; my English is good, I learn fast. Now I live with my sister, her daughter, and my three kids.

My sister found me a job where she used to work, as a cashier in a 99-cent store. They treated me nice. The job was part time with minimum salary; I got paid $150 a week. In a typical day, I used to work from three to eight in the afternoon, with one day off a week. The only holidays I had off were Christmas and New Year's.

I loved my job because I knew a lot of people. I used to talk with everybody. We talked about what happened in the *novelas*, and about their lives. Sometimes we talked about what happened in *el barrio*. I talk with a lot of people from *el barrio*, Puerto Ricans, Dominicans, Africans, Mexicans, and a lot of times people from Panama that I didn't know were Panamanians. I still walk there today, and my daughter gets mad because in one block I stop like five times to talk to different people.

Now I work in a hotel, cleaning the rooms. When I went back to visit the 99-cent store, everybody came to me and asked why I left. They said that the store wasn't the same without me. It feels great to be loved.

Breathing My Own Death

Asbestos removal worker

COUNTRY OF ORIGIN: Czech Republic

MY FAMILY WAS POOR, WITH SEVEN BROTHERS AND SIX SISTERS, and I left my home at sixteen, working on farms and for anyone who needed help with anything. Then I found my passion, working as a blacksmith for so long I don't even remember. About seven years ago, I moved my family from the Czech Republic to the United States. I didn't want my two daughters to struggle like me.

Any male that enters the United States from my country usually ends up in construction work. I had many jobs in construction, but they all used me because they knew my immigration status. Sometimes they wouldn't even pay me; if they did, it was very little. We had to buy our own tools. I could never complain to anyone, because even now I know only about five words in English.

A Czech friend who lives near me told me that I should do what he does, removing asbestos. As soon as he said that scary word, I thought of my health. But how could I refuse, when he said $38 plus benefits? The dark cloud of asbestos left my head; money was what I concentrated on.

To get into asbestos removal, every state requires a different test. I took the test in Polish, but my Polish wasn't great either. I took it three times before I passed. I am so glad it's over; at 45, I cannot study anymore. But my daughter says I have golden hands, because without them we would be nothing.

I can't say that I hate my job. I can speak Czech there; that's a big relief. I get good money, and my family has great benefits. Still, things that are too good usually have a bad side. Sometimes I have to work for fourteen hours straight, to finish the job. I have to wear a special mask every minute that I work with asbestos—at least that's the law, but my company doesn't follow it. If we had an inspection, the company would have many violations.

It is not nice to see my co-workers who have been in the asbestos field for some time. They cough so much that they start to choke. Many have died or are seriously ill. I think a lot about my own health, and whether I will reach my hopes and dreams. In five years, I see myself back in my home-land, with my wife and my own house; my kids will come and visit us. But for now, I'll just stick to breathing my own death.

A Language Is Like a Bridge

Hospital clerk

COUNTRY OF ORIGIN: Cameroon

YOU KNOW, LIFE IS ABOUT SACRIFICE AND COMMITMENT. I prioritize every day. It takes lot of courage and determination to work all night and stay in school all day. I manage by the grace of God.

My job sent me here in 1993 to be a secretary at the United Nations, doing stenography for the nation of Cameroon. I had been doing it for many years, in Africa and also in China for seven years. When I transferred to the United States it was a big accomplishment. It was good working with ambassadors, the minister of foreign affairs for my country, and other foreign affairs officials of the United Nations, solving diplomatic issues.

I was married and had three kids when I came to New York, and I had the fourth child here. After my five-year contract expired, I was supposed to go back to Cameroon, but I refused, so my children could continue school here. Taking my daughter back to Cameroon was going to create a big mess for her education. When I worked in China, she went to a Chinese school. In New York, I first registered her in a French school, but it was too expensive. Why transfer a child to a Chinese school, a French school, an English school, and then what?

My husband died about five years ago. It has been very hard to take care of the children since then. My brothers and sisters are all in Cameroon. I miss them so bad, sometimes it makes me cry.

French is my first language, and when I first came I wasn't very fluent in English. A language is like a bridge. In China, you need to know Chinese; in the United States, English. This is the country of opportunity, so I said, "Well, I'm not going to let the opportunity go by." I decided to go back to school, to improve my English and learn a skill needed in this country. I'm a nursing student at Lehman College during the day, but at night I work at the Columbia pediatrics hospital as a unit assistant.

I'm happy with my job. I love children, and here I see babies being born every night. But I will be even happier when I finish and become a full time nurse. That's my goal, to become a talented African lady, willing to help and give care to all patients.

War Drove Me from Happiness

Taxi driver

COUNTRY OF ORIGIN: Afghanistan

FROM FIVE A.M. TO FIVE P.M. in Manhattan, Long Island, Brooklyn, and Queens I pick up and drop off my passengers. On sunny, icy, windy days, I have to drive to stay alive.

For fifteen years I was far from my wife, three sons, and three daughters in Afghanistan. I lost two brothers in 1990, in the war there. My mother, father, and sisters passed away because of sickness. I lost my youngest brother in 2002 in Pakistan, because high-quality medicine was not available.

People frame big dreams, but the image inside that frame never appears. I came to the U.S. as an international student for three months, but when the economic and political situation in Afghanistan got worse, I decided not to go back. I started by giving out flyers on the street and living with a relative. After a year, I started driving a taxi, and I have worked at that for thirteen years.

I worked and worked, but you cannot earn happiness with money. The smile of your children brings on your face a smile, and I had no family beside me. Here you think first of yourself, but in Afghanistan you think of community and family before yourself. Everyone knows each other; every morning when the sun rises, they pass peace upon each other.

I always worried about my family, knowing it would be very hard for them. My wife moved from Afghanistan to Pakistan for their safety, and I sent them money every month. I did not have papers or my green card, so I wasn't able to sponsor them to come here, and I did not have permission to travel. After 1979 there was civil war in Afghanistan, and I wrote to the immigration office about how difficult it would be to go back. I got accepted for asylum, but as the clock hands moved, my children were growing up as orphans. I hardly could talk with them once or twice a year.

In 2001, I finally finished my children's paperwork, and now it has been almost four years that they have lived with me. I am happy that they are safe from wars, but it's human nature to want to be somewhere else. Living in the land of opportunities, I miss the manager's job I had in Afghanistan. I still support my two brothers' widows and their eight orphaned children. I hope for a proud future for our children. But words are cheap, and I am a man of action. What I have been and done will help me wish for a new dream.

International Business

Manager, beauty supply store

COUNTRY OF ORIGIN: Ivory Coast

I CAME TO THE UNITED STATES, IN SEPTEMBER 1994, wanting a higher education. After getting my high school diploma in Africa, I thought going to college here and learning English would be a good opportunity. I didn't complain about my life. I was 23 years old. My wife and I had a clothing store that she managed while I was at school, and we had a son. But I was curious to discover the United States.

When I arrived, I faced financial problems so I didn't go straight to college. After three days, I had a job. I lived with my brother-in-law and worked with his company, distributing flyers in apartment buildings from six in the morning until seven at night. It was hard, especially in the cold.

After saving some money I went to university in Pennsylvania, and a year later I changed to Borough of Manhattan Community College. After that, I stopped; I didn't have enough money and had to go to work again. Even though I didn't know much about it, I became a construction worker, working on Elmundo, a big store where you can find almost everything, electronic stuff, clothes, shoes, and food products. After I couldn't take the hard work of construction anymore, I ended up washing dishes in a restaurant at Grand Central Station. I worked from two in the morning to one in the afternoon.

My wife had a beauty supply store, and later on I helped her manage it. The business grew; now we get products from the companies instead of from the Chinese, and some other stores even get products from us. Meanwhile, I went to LaGuardia Community College, where I now have fifty credits in international business.

I go to work and school, take care of my kids, and take care of my family in my country. Life is not easy.

Waiting to See You Again

School bus attendant

COUNTRY OF ORIGIN: Peru

IT'S ALREADY TEN P.M.; IF I'M LUCKY, I'll be at home around midnight. I'm still waiting for the bus. This is a quiet and dark place, and it's snowing; I can hardly feel my hands and face. The solitude makes me remember everything as if it was yesterday. "Mamita, regresa pronto," were my daughter's last words when we were saying goodbye in the airport. My son didn't even look at me; he put his head down and I saw tears running down his little face. That was when I came from Peru, five years ago.

In Peru I worked as a secretary for a prestigious company. The work was good. Even though I was a single mother, I never struggled to give my two kids what they needed. But the company went into bankruptcy and closed. I couldn't find another job like that one.

My niece had already been in this country seven years, managing a laundromat. She offered to help me find a job here to assure the well-being of my kids. The father of my children could take care of them while I was in this country. A few months later, I left my house and everything that I knew and loved.

Working at the laundromat with my niece was stressful and hard. I would open it on weekends and work from seven a.m. to nine p.m. I slept in her living room and paid a rent of $450 per month. Her house was in Jamaica and the laundromat in Rockaway; I had to wait at the bus stop half an hour in winter. Six months later I left that house and quit that job.

Now I work every morning in a school bus for handicapped children of all ages. My job is to help them get in and out and to maintain order in the bus. It's hard with the teenage kids; they are stronger and very disrespectful. But I get benefits that I didn't have in the laundromat and enough money to maintain my kids in Peru.

I still dream about bringing them to this country, after I get my residency. My son and daughter are young adults and I know they need me more than ever. One day when my son answered the phone, I didn't recognize his voice; I thought it was some friend of his dad. My daughter graduates this year from high school. I'm so proud of her, but I feel sad that I won't be at her graduation day. I will never know if I made the best decision, but we all need to sacrifice something to get something.

A Needle Through My Finger

Sewing machine operator

COUNTRY OF ORIGIN: Ecuador

I WORK IN A FACTORY WHERE THEY MAKE TARPS FOR THE ARMY. I get paid seven dollars per hour, working Monday through Saturday, from seven a.m. to five-thirty p.m., and they do not count the half hour for lunch. Even though I am legal and it's a lot of hours, I don't get paid overtime and I get no benefits. But I don't want to leave; the bosses and co-workers are nice, and the job is stable.

The job I do is extremely hard and tiring. I work sitting all day and the tarps I sew are so heavy. In my first days, my arms ached a lot; if someone touched me on the arm I screamed because it hurt. We don't use uniforms and safety equipment, and my shoes and clothes have damage because of oil from the machines. A co-worker is now in the hospital because he got sick, and I am afraid the materials at this job will make me sick too. Something like a ball is growing in my shoulder. I went to the hospital, but I don't know yet what it is.

This work is worse than the first job I had, as a sewing machine operator in a sweater factory, when I first came here in 1994 from Ecuador. There I worked the same amount of hours, but at least I got paid overtime. The bosses were nice; they never got mad when I didn't go to work. At the time I was pregnant, and they allowed me to work until two or three weeks before I gave birth to my son, who now is five years old. One time at that job, I was sewing a sweater and thinking about something else, and the needle went through my fingernail to the other side of my finger. I didn't go to the hospital, because I don't like how slowly the doctors help people there. Instead, a co-worker took out the needle with tweezers. It hurt me a lot, but thank God the needle didn't break in the middle of my finger.

The money that I get paid here doesn't help a lot to maintain a family. Our children always need something; sometimes there is not enough money, and it makes us feel bad. I hope that our work and the education we are giving to our children will help. I don't want them to work the way people like me do, without a specialty that can help many people.

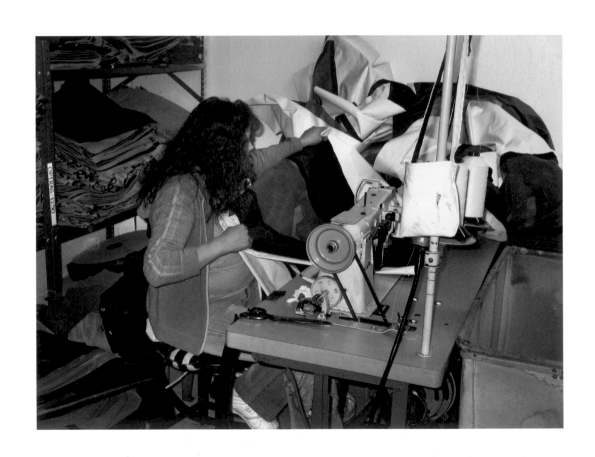

Please God, Don't Cry Today

Car wash worker

COUNTRY OF ORIGIN: Dominican Republic

NOT AGAIN! IT'S RAINING FOR THE THIRD TIME THIS WEEK; I'll have to take the day off. The water steals my job; my tips vanish in the air. Everyone who owns a car goes out on rainy days so the water can do its work for free. They do not see that I need to wash their car to survive.

Right now I am waiting for the cars to come. I don't use technology to do my job. My hands move up and down with a wet sop towel. It keeps my hands and body exercising, and I'm healthy, thanks to that and all the food that I eat. But I have to pay my dentist bill.

I came ten years ago looking for a better future and I'm still looking for it. Growing up in Brooklyn with the Dominican community, it was hard to learn good English. I know English, but not what's necessary to work at a law firm or at an executive office.

"Hey, *plátano*, the next car is mine!" my co-worker screams, as if I would get mad. All right, take it. "One day I'll own this place, you'll see." This cat does not believe me, and laughs at me. Not really, he laughs with me. Well, one day I'll buy this car wash. At my job, there isn't any way to go up. Either you own the place or you are a worker.

I'm working on the American dream. I'm legal, I have the green card. I'm saving money; in a regular week I make from $420 to $450, but at Christmas the tips I make are a lot more. Some woman once told me, "Work in a car wash equals a poor man." But I live well, and most important, I am saving more money than she imagines. I am twenty-two right now and I'm thankful for all the opportunities that I have. "*Gracias Dios por otro día de vida y de trabajo.*"

How I miss the sunny days in the Dominican Republic. Back then I didn't care if it rained. In twenty years, I'll be living back in Los Minas, my hometown, which is special in every way. I'll buy a huge house with a *balcón*, and two more cars. That is the place where I would rather be, instead of here at the car wash, where I keep on praying, "Please God, don't cry today, let me work the whole day."

Make Your Nails Pretty Is My Job

Manicurist

COUNTRY OF ORIGIN: China

NAILS ARE A PART OF THE BODY, AND ALSO A PART OF MY LIFE. I manicure people's nails. It is comfortable work, but the chemicals are dangerous. I cover my nose, mouth, and hands, but it is not enough to make me not smell them. Sometimes during the job I can't breathe easily, and I cough a lot.

I am a woman without the education to get a better job. They trained me how to manicure nails, but I don't have a license for it. It took me three months to learn the basic steps. I get tips from my job, but not that much. If it is a busy day, then I get more; not, I get only a little. I don't get benefits.

It is not easy to talk with the customers. I feel sad when they have a bad attitude talking to me. I am like a slave in their eyes; they think my job is for low level and poor people.

Before this, I was a supermarket cashier. It was hard for me to stand all day, without any breaks. My body always hurt. Because I was tired, sometimes I miscounted the food and got less money, so at the end of the day the computer and the actual money didn't match. To make sure it was the same, I had to take it out of my pay. Once I got paid only $30 of my money, and I made only about $65 a day.

I don't have any children yet, because my husband and I are afraid that we don't have enough money to take care of a child. My entire family is still in China. I'm here illegally, so there is little chance for me to travel back and see my parents. Now is the time for me to save money and work hard. I feel sorry that I came here to struggle. I don't know what I will do next.

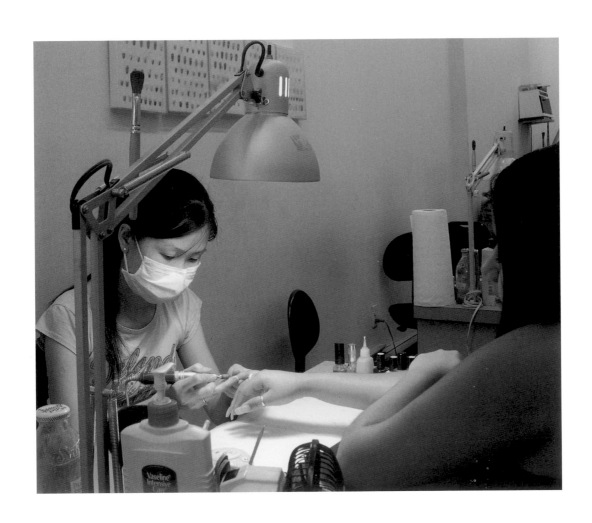

You Have to Do Something Against Yourself

Photographer

COUNTRY OF ORIGIN: Poland

I COME FROM SOPOT, A BEAUTIFUL POLISH CITY OF ARTISTS. I left with my sister in 1991, two years after communism, to go to our father, who was documented in the U.S. I took all my films and my music collection and sent twenty-seven boxes of books. I wanted to build my own little world, where I could feel the way I felt in my country.

My beginning in the U.S. was a fight for everything. I lived in the East Village with no electricity, gas, or kitchen. I said to myself, "Is this Manhattan?" I didn't go out of my apartment for three months. I counted every day of my misery. My family wanted me to work immediately, but I revolted. I went to a school for immigrants, and later to Hunter College, where I learned English. Then I took photography classes. At times, I walked seventy streets from school to home just to save a dollar fifty. Almost everything I bought on the street.

I worked in a laundromat from five to ten p.m., for five dollars an hour. I had another job, as a porter in a condominium, from midnight to eight a.m., for seven dollars an hour. I slept only two hours, then went to the third job, where I delivered sandwiches to offices, for three dollars an hour plus tips. My last physical job was repairing elevators in rich buildings, eight hours a day in foil-covered dusty elevators. Americans would get forty dollars an hour for the job, and I got twelve.

Walking on the streets, I felt sick to see so many interesting faces that could be photographed. So I took pictures. I had a darkroom in my apartment; for six hours a day I developed pictures of people, and then sold them. Working for free for a small newspaper, I became known in the Polish community. I displayed my photos at exhibitions and was noticed by the editor of the biggest Polish news agency in New York, where I work to this day. Later, I got to know an interior designer and began shooting his projects before and after. Finally, I started wedding photography. Now I decide what time I want to get up, how much work I do, and how much money I get.

Sometimes, when you can't live from doing what you love, you have to do something against yourself to survive. There was a huge transition in my life, from the time when I worked physically and dreamed about photography to a time when I left everything to do what I have always dreamed of. I'm glad that I live here. New York became my city.

Move Many Things, and My Hands Are Numb

Department manager, wholesale company

COUNTRY OF ORIGIN: China

I WAS A BUSINESSMAN IN CHINA, BUT I LOST MY BUSINESS. My friends suggested that I go to the United States, telling me that dollars were worth much more than our money. I knew that I would have hardship, but I wanted to support my family. I spent a lot to come here, borrowing much money from relatives and friends. So I had a lot of pressure when I first came here, and my life was hard.

It was difficult to find a good job, because I wasn't good at English. My friend asked me to work in a wholesale company, carrying goods such as rice, beer, and water. After six years I am now a departmental manager, directing workers to put goods in a warehouse. It isn't easy to direct thirty workers to get their work done. Sometimes we have arguments because they don't listen. I also have to carry goods myself, and after my co-workers leave I count the inventory. It is a long day, from seven in the morning to nine at night, and I am always last to leave.

Even though I am a manager, I don't get high pay and benefits. I don't have vacation and I don't get paid for holidays. A big problem is that I don't have any health insurance. I often get injured but don't get treated. My back is always painful, and I spend much money to see doctors. My work-place is in a basement with many goods, and a lot of garbage on the floors. Even though the smell is so bad, we always have lunch there.

My job is dangerous. One day I was hurt badly when a lot of rice fell down and covered me while I was getting my lunch. My co-workers were very worried as they hurried to remove it, and I was sent to the hospital immediately. Luckily, I only hurt my legs and didn't spend much time in the hospital.

My goal is to bring my children and wife here and earn enough money to support them. I don't want my children to do the same job as me.

Faking Smiles or Making Smiles?

Dental technician

COUNTRY OF ORIGIN: Colombia

Tsssss! tssss!" is the sound you'll hear when you come to see me do part of my job. I am the one that puts the smiles on your grandpa and grandma. I work as a dental technician, making the porcelain dentures, crowns, bridges, and framework that get sent to dentists, who give the finished work to patients.

I'm 54 years old and I come from Colombia. I've been in this country already for six years, and I love it here. Nowadays, who doesn't want to come to the U.S.? This is the country of opportunities and cultures.

I've been working in this field for thirty years. My father was also a dental technician; when I was young, I saw him do his job and got interested in it. In this job you get to be very handy, and I liked that. I always was passionate about art and studied it some when I was young. Someday I will spend more time painting, one of the things I like most.

Right now I'm working to open my own business. My last job, working for a company, was very tiring; I worked Monday to Saturday from eight in the morning until about eleven at night. I didn't have any time except Sundays to spend at home with my family. Now I work ten hours a day, and in the future, I see myself doing better at my job and working less.

Plants, Planes, and Passengers

Airport employee, flower shop worker

COUNTRY OF ORIGIN: Brazil

I N BRAZIL I USED TO WORK AFTER SCHOOL IN A BAKERY, to pay for the things I wanted. One day in 1980, my best friend asked me if I wanted to come with her illegally to the United States, so I could do better than that. Two weeks later I said goodbye to my family. It was really hard for them to see me go, because we knew I could die on the way.

I went to Rio de Janeiro first, and then took a plane to Mexico. For two months I worked as a waitress in a restaurant there, so I could collect more money, learn some language, and, most important, be near the border between the U.S. and Mexico. Finally, I had the guts to cross it. Thanks to my mother's side of my family I have blue eyes, and I dyed my hair blond. My false documentation worked like a charm, the officer at the border did not ask me any questions, and I made it past the border with no problem.

My friend and I went to California and worked in a flower shop. Portuguese is similar to Spanish, so I learned Spanish pretty quickly. I used to make six dollars an hour, making flower arrangements and taking care of the plants and flowers. I did not have any benefits, but since I was really responsible I never had to worry about job security. In 1986, I married the owner of the flower shop.

My husband woke up one day and decided to come to New York, leaving the shop in the care of his brother and my friend. We opened a flower shop in Astoria, where there was a large community of Brazilians. My husband is documented, so I was able to get my documents, too. I always thought I could do better, so I took an intensive English class. After I passed the GED, I was able to go to college, where I studied liberal arts. Recently I started working at John F. Kennedy Airport, helping people who do not speak English; on the weekends, I help my husband in the shop.

One Hundred Packets of Freedom

Food preparation worker

COUNTRY OF ORIGIN: Bangladesh

I CAME TO THE U.S.A. IN 2001 FROM BANGLADESH to join my husband, because I wanted a better life. I didn't know anyone, and everything was totally different here. I miss my relatives, but I had to come for my children's education; the most important thing is the English language. We are happy to be together, and my husband helps me take care of my children.

One month after we came here, my husband took us to a friend's house and I met his friend's wife. I was bored at home all alone, with nothing to do when the children were in school. So she came to my house and took me to a food factory, where a lot of people from India and other countries were working. She asked her boss to give me a job, and a week later, the boss called me.

I work at home. My responsibility is to go to the factory to get the supplies, bring them home, make the Indian food *somucha* (it's a vegetable pie), and deliver it when they need it. Making the food is easy; the hard part is bringing it and taking it back.

With my co-workers and my boss I have a friendly relationship. I tried to learn how to speak Hindi, because the boss is from India and she speaks Hindi. Sometimes when they are busy, though, they give all the people who work there a hard time. When the Muslim holiday came, they forced every person to make one hundred packets of somucha a day. Each packet has fifty somucha inside and it takes around one and a half hours to make. Can you imagine that? How can people do it?

They give us too little, only 75 cents for each packet. If I make three hundred packets, I get around two hundred dollars. I do not get any benefits from this job, not even health benefits. Sometimes my boss gives us gifts at the end of the year.

I do this hard job because I want to help my husband, and to pass time while my children are at school. My husband works at a printing press, and he has a better salary. If I worked in a factory, I couldn't go anywhere whenever I felt like it. With this job, I have freedom.

Freezing Hands and Face

Supermarket worker

COUNTRY OF ORIGIN: China

W HEN I FIRST CAME HERE IN 1995, I didn't have a job in my country. I always heard that the U.S. had many easy jobs, and I thought I should give it a try, at least. If I stayed in my country, my whole life would be the same. I wanted to see some good changes.

I didn't speak English or know anything about the U.S., so I didn't have a lot of choice when I first arrived. My brother found me a job selling fruit in the street for a supermarket. I am still doing this job today.

Many people think this is an easy job, and not dangerous. This is not true; the fruits are very heavy to carry out. The most terrible times are in winter, with my freezing hands and face. Go try it out, staying outside for thirteen hours.

It is also hard to communicate with customers. Working in Chinatown is very different; there are a lot of Chinese, but also many Americans. Sometimes I find it interesting to talk with customers, but sometimes they are very tough on me.

Every day I have to wake up at six a.m., because I live in Queens, far away from Chinatown. I get one day off a week, not enough time to spend with my family and relax. Usually, on the day I don't work I just sleep the whole day. People are surprised, but I am just too tired.

As a supermarket worker, I don't have benefits such as health care or sick-day pay. I get about $500 per week—not bad, but I do a lot to get it. My boss is my brother. I hate to say that; how could a brother give me this job, when he is the boss? But he treats me well. He has worked hard to get to this level, and he must have a lot of problems to keep this supermarket good.

I hope I can go back to my country, but I have not saved enough. My children are still small, and this job gives me the money to take care of them well. I feel happy to serve others, but sad for myself. My future will be my children and this job. I deserve to be called a hard worker.

Bleach on Color Clothes

Laundromat worker

COUNTRY OF ORIGIN: Indonesia

EIGHT YEARS I'VE BEEN WORKING IN THIS LAUNDROMAT, washing and drying the clothes of customers. It is an easy job, because washing clothes is what I do for my family all the time. The only differences now are that I have to wash many more clothes every day, and I am washing for other people.

I don't have long work hours, only eight hours each day and six days a week. We don't have any vacations, holidays, or health benefits; I have to go to work when I'm sick. But in this job I can meet many new people and wash my own clothes for free. The boss is a nice person, which is why I have stayed for so long. Each morning, my co-workers take turns buying breakfast for each other and eating together. We help each other when we are tired of washing clothes, and we collaborate. I don't have to worry about getting hurt.

Even though the job is easy, I always make some mistakes. I might lose one or two of the customers' clothes when I'm not careful. Once I accidentally put bleach on clothes that had color; the colors went away and some of the delicate clothes were ripped. When the customer came to pick up the clothes, I told her what had happened. She screamed at me in front of everybody; I wanted to dig a hole and hide. I had to pay a hundred dollars to her to calm her down.

I knew a little English when I was in Indonesia, and after about ten years here, it has advanced. A medium English level is fine to know what to tell customers when they drop off the clothes.

In Indonesia, I was an accountant in a television factory. I came here to seek a better life. However, even with a higher salary, life here isn't as good as in Indonesia, where everything is much cheaper. There, I had a bigger house and even a housekeeper; here we can only rent a house. I don't take care of my family's expenses; my husband earns much more than I do. Four years ago, I brought my daughter here, and last year I brought my son. It would be better if I could bring my parents, too. But I am happy that my family can be together.

Out of the Black Hole

Independent salesman

COUNTRY OF ORIGIN: China

IF ANYONE ASKED ME WHAT I WILL DO IN THE FUTURE, I would answer, "I don't know." I will let time decide. Maybe in a month I will believe in something, and work hard to achieve it. Or it may take years for me to think about my future again.

Just a few years ago, my thoughts were different. I had a bright future, and a family in China. The warmth of having a wife and son made me want to give everything to make their life comfortable and happy. However, I was a teacher; my salary was enough to survive, but not to make any progress. I had to find a job with a much greater income, for what I had planned for them: a house for the three of us, a car to take us on vacations. I decided to migrate to the U.S. to seek a better economic situation.

Things didn't go as well as I had planned. My wife did not understand the idea of my departure. She didn't want me to leave her and our young son alone in China. Poor or rich, as long as the whole family was together, she would be thankful. But I crossed my heart, swallowed the teardrops, and flew to the U.S. Not long after, a message came to me across the sea that my wife had left the family, leaving our son with my parents.

Heart broken, dreams deferred, brains scrambled, I felt helpless and depressed. I had no money, so I had to take any job available. I worked in a restaurant and a factory more than thirteen hours per day, for really low pay. I didn't care how hard I worked; the happiness and satisfaction that people should have from a job became less important to me.

The idea of supporting my son got me out of that black hole. I had a plan: save money first, then start my own business. So after three years working like a dog, I finally bought a car and started my business. Now I drive my little car to many different factories, to sell everything that people need, like food and home and office supplies. I am the boss and the only worker. I love my job, even though it doesn't provide me a lot of money and benefits. Instead, I get freedom and happiness. For now, I send money back home monthly, for my son to go to school. And the freedom and comfort of being my own boss is bringing me back a little more spirit and life.

Woodhaven Boulevard

Newspaper hawker

COUNTRY OF ORIGIN: Bangladesh

"NEW YORK TIMES! DAILY NEWS! NEW YORK POST! NEWSPAPERS!" I call this out from 5:30 in the morning until late in the afternoons, from a sidewalk on Woodhaven Boulevard. Seven days a week I stand between two huge and dangerous highways, no matter if it's raining or hot as hell, Christmas or any other holiday. When I see that the light is going to turn red and cars are preparing to stop, I need to be fast and have my eyes really open. Those red lights are the only chances I have to sell the newspapers.

I came to this country in my early fifties, from a city in Bangladesh where I lived with my wife, my daughter, and her two sons. We were a middle-class family, but the most important thing for us was that we were happy and united. When my daughter died in an accident, I and my wife stayed alone with my grandchildren. They were still young, and I didn't know what to do. Months later, I used all the money I had saved for many years and came here with them and my wife. Because of my age, my lack of English, and my immigration status I couldn't find a better job than an office cleaner—or this job.

This job is hard and crazy. I have seen many traffic accidents, and sometimes the police call me to testify. But I have lost any fear of the cars and the streets. People treat me the way they want. Some of them are polite, nice people who give me a dollar and tell me to keep the change. Others are rude; if the light is already changing to green, they just throw the money in the highway and make me go running after the 25 cents. Not so nice, eh? There's no lunchtime, no help, no benefits. If I get sick, I still need to find a way to get money.

Don't think that because I am a little bit older I don't have the strength and the agility of a young man, seeing who needs a newspaper and running between cars all day. I get strength from the hope to give my grandchildren and wife a better life. I get agility from the desire and need to put food on the table every night. This is the way I live and I don't complain. At my 56 years, I am still running on the streets like a teenager; many people of my age would like to say the same. I just hope God gives me more strength and health to keep watching over my grandsons. In the end, they are the ones who complete my life and make me feel useful.

Your Body Becomes a Machine

Welder

COUNTRY OF ORIGIN: Dominican Republic

THE NEW YORK OF POSTCARDS, that's the New York your eyes and mind see, but it's not the one you live. As an immigrant, you don't belong to those great buildings, except as the one that mops the floor. You didn't belong to the society that made the buildings. This is a New York where you still face discrimination.

Thirty years ago, when I came to this country from the Dominican Republic, I wanted to study. I had come with a professional skill, welding. So I studied and worked, but I was disappointed. The job I did gave me no time for college. We worked under very harmful conditions. The environment purification system was not adequate; workers faced lung problems, and some even died.

People think discrimination is being called a name, but that's just one form of it. Discrimination is also being paid less than you deserve, or working in horrible conditions. We were uninformed, unaware of the benefits we should have had. Not speaking the language, I had no other alternative.

With what I do, you don't usually need to speak English, so I observed rather than spoke. Observation is one of the beauties life gives you. Throughout my work experience, I've learned that you need to see life from various points of view. You need to value your life more than your job. You need to be more independent and not work for other people so much.

Now I work ten hours a day in another company, with two hours of commuting. After thirty years of working with metals, your body becomes a machine, designed to do the same things every day. My back is tired; x-rays have damaged my sight. But this company takes care of the environment and its workers. I work in comfort, and have great health insurance. The wage is not bad, though I feel I should earn more for this profession. Things have turned much better, but not completely.

I feel satisfied for myself, but not with the system. This is a modern slavery, not only from white to black, but also from the oligarchy to the common people, from the millionaires to the rest of us. The government becomes part of the system. Instead of being chained, we "get paid"— but the money just passes through our hands. Spending money and having little to save becomes a habit, and eventually you can never progress.

Sacrifice, the Meaning of Life

Restaurant chef

COUNTRY OF ORIGIN: China

COMING BACK TO THE APARTMENT AFTER A TIRING DAY and making myself comfortable on the bed, I wouldn't even bother turning on the light. Breathing softly, stretching my body, I would relax. After a few minutes I headed to the shower, getting rid of all the sweat, oil, and stress from working in a Chinese restaurant as a chef. Then I would pick up the phone and call my family. It was afternoon in China at midnight in the United States, which was usually the time I came home from work. My wife's familiar voice made me feel not so lonely anymore, even though I lived alone. My sons came and talked on the phone, too. Their "Hi, Dad" and "How are you, Dad"—all those simple sentences people might not pay attention to—became my most powerful stress relief. The bed felt much more comfortable; my eyes closed by themselves. The call ended soon, but I was satisfied. I would switch on the tape player and familiar music would fill the room. Then I read the newspaper under the dim bed lamp. That night, I would have a sweet dream.

When I first came to the U.S. eleven years ago, the only job available for a Chinese immigrant with no English was working in a Chinese restaurant. I started as a dishwasher, then helped the chef, learning skills through watching and with help from a coworker. Eventually, I became a kitchen chef myself. Even for the chef, the work is tiring and stressful, and I got no benefits. However, I was happy to have a job. My coworkers in the restaurant treated each other okay, maybe because we came from the same country and share the same language.

As long as my salary is enough to support my family in China with a little left to save, I am satisfied. I have three sons with bright futures. I was willing to give up years of seeing them in order to immigrate to the United States, a place unknown, and help them have a better life. Eleven years later my family was able to come to the U.S., too. The joy of the whole family uniting was indescribable. I may not have shown much of that excitement, but I laughed out loud during my dreams. My job hasn't changed much. The salary is about $40,000, which covers my family's daily needs, and through my wife's help, the burden of supporting the family is much lighter. My goal for now is to save money and buy a house for us, so the kids can gather in our living room, watch a basketball game together, play chess, and taste the delicious meal prepared by their mom. Life will be better, much better.

The Truth Behind the American Dream

Waiter

COUNTRY OF ORIGIN: Mexico

Y OU COULD WORK VERY HARD, YOU COULD TRY YOUR BEST, and still there is no guarantee that you will get the American dream. I've been in this country for seventeen years, and still I feel like nothing has happened. I'm doing the same thing, trying to survive here and sending money to my family so they can survive over there.

When I was in Mexico I had a job as a construction worker. The pay wasn't good, and the conditions were horrible. When I was sixteen, I had my son and my need for money became stronger. Many people were coming to the United States and I saw that as my only way out. I planned to come, save money, and then go back to Mexico, where I could buy a taxi and support my new family.

When I got to this country, I cleaned kitchens as hot as saunas, washed dishes at a busy restaurant, polished floors in supermarkets, and finally worked as a busboy. Years later, my brother got me a job as a room service attendant at one of the nicest hotels in the city. The interaction with so many people always kept me happy there, and one day I told my supervisor that I wanted to work in private parties at the hotel. "You don't have the right presentation for that position," she said. She didn't think I had the skills, even though I had worked in restaurants for almost ten years; but she thought that the new white guys, whom I taught how to carry a tray, did have them. Days after this discussion, I got fired for no reason; but because I didn't have papers I couldn't say anything. Right now I work 45 to 55 hours a week as a waiter in a restaurant downtown. I have no benefits and I don't get paid overtime, but I can't risk my job. I have to send money to my mother and my son.

My son is the only reason I regret my decision to come here. We talk on the phone, but he feels like a stranger. He has problems with his stepfather. I didn't want to get involved, but I should have been there to support him, even by phone. Now our relationship is growing.

My American dream was to become a food and beverage manager at a hotel. I took classes in English and literature, and I have an associates degree in hospitality and tourism. But I will be working as a waiter until I go back to my country. This country gives you many opportunities, but to get them, you have to force yourself, and be persistent. You have to be ready to feel lonely and depressed; you won't find here that warm feeling of being at home.

Pathologies Are the Same Everywhere

Dentist

COUNTRY OF ORIGIN: Colombia

I USED TO COME TO THE U.S. FREQUENTLY, as a tourist and for business. I liked the system. Of course, then I had money to rent a good car, go shopping, and eat in good restaurants. When I came from Colombia four years ago, it was very different. I had to work in anything to survive.

I'm a dentist. I went to dentistry school in Colombia for five years, then specialized in maxillofacial surgery for four years. I was successful, but I had the opportunity to start a construction company. That was a good business and a comfortable life, but changes in the country led the company to bankruptcy. I thought the U.S. would give me at least the opportunity of surviving.

It took me a while to get my first job here, distributing flyers for about a year. But anyone could do that job; I thought I should use my knowledge and do something I like. It was difficult to work in business, because I didn't have a formal education in that field. But I did have education, knowledge, and professional skills as a dentist, and I thought I could probably get my license here.

Then I realized that for me that was almost impossible. At over 45, I didn't want to go to a university more years to learn things I already had done. Getting a dentistry degree here can cost more than $100,000, and I had no credit. I don't speak English or have legal immigration status.

I tried to get a job as a dental assistant, but employers thought that position was too low for my resumé. So I talked to other immigrants who had been professionals about how to work here without a license. The license is important to promote yourself, but what really matters is knowledge. Sickness and pathologies are the same everywhere. To work in the mouth of a Chinese or American person, the procedures are the same.

Unlicensed dentists work at their apartments or get private offices not open to the public. They create chains of patients who speak their language, trying to give them excellent service at a lower cost. I've been working this way for three years now. What I'm doing, I do right, from the professional point of view. But from another point of view, my job is illegal.

Acknowledgments

Students whose text or photograph (sometimes both) appears in this book

Asma Akter
Kariela Almonte
Damima Bakayoko
Jackie Bao
Diego Barragán
Sandra Barrera
Oscar Beltrán
Alex Benitez
Dong Ming Chen
Hui Zhen Chen
Eric Dai
Djara Diabate
Angy Gonzalez
Katerina Habanova
Li Wu Huang
Ling Jun Jiang
Nergies Khawaja
Mariajosé Lago
Dong Mei Li
Fen Li
He Li

Li Li
Josine Lin
Jonathan López
Diana Marin
Judyta Mirowska
Jessica Orellana
Jodai Patrick
Wei Quan
Carlos Quiroz
Carla Robles
Miguel Rodríquez
Peach Shupongpun
Dong Xue

Photos on pages 7, 9, 19, 25, 33, 35, 43, and 59 by Rosa Fernández

Other student participants in the project

Cristian Acevedo
Omar Alcázar
Kazi Anisuzzaman
Sami Aqel
Henrique Avellar
Thuza Aye
Kamil Betko
Thiago Cleim
Aida Diallo
Lan Mei Fu
Vanessa Jean
Awa Kaba
Salvador Narciso
Luis Nivellera
Sarah Philippeaux
Fior Rodríguez
Gino San Martín
Ronald Sandoval
Rama Sylla
Ronald Tavárez
Salif Tounkara
Esteban Vidal
Xiang Wang
Fu Ying
Serena Zheng

TEACHERS AND MENTORS

James Duval
Manhattan International High School (student teacher)

Annie Gwynne-Vaughan
Manhattan International High School

Noreen Perlmutter
International High School at LaGuardia Community College

Jaime Permuth
Photographer and teaching artist, Elders Share the Arts

Justine Stehle
National Center for Creative Aging, Elders Share the Arts, Brooklyn

Andrew Turner
International High School at LaGuardia Community College

Christopher Wilson
Brooklyn International High School

Carolyn Zablotny
National Center for Creative Aging, Elders Share the Arts, Brooklyn

CREDITS

Photography editor: Barbara Cervone
Story editor: Kathleen Cushman
Production editor: Rosa Fernández

*All proceeds from the sale of this book will support additional
projects by students in New York City's schools for newcomers.*

I HAD WAITED SO LONG TO COME TO AMERICA and rejoin with my husband. It was a night in October 1998 when the immigration office in Guan Dong informed me that our application had finally been accepted. When we arrived at the New York City airport at 10:00 pm on December 30, 1998, I was exuberant and nervous. My husband had left me for ten years. Now was my chance to see him again.

– Unemployed

THIS YEAR I AM 76 YEARS OLD. In the year 1978, my youngest brother got me a visa for coming to the United States. I boarded the airplane in Hong Kong, it stopped in Korea, and then it flew all the way to JFK. After my brother picked up me from the airport, we took a taxi to his place. I couldn't stop thinking of my family that was still in China, my wife and two daughters.

– Retired chef